Simple Delights

HERBS & SPICES

Simple Delights

HERBS & SPICES

Salamander Books Limited
LONDON

A SALAMANDER BOOK

Published by Salamander Books Limited
129-137 York Way
London N7 9LG
United Kingdom

1 3 5 7 9 8 6 4 2

Distributed by Random House Value Publishing, Inc.
40 Engelhard Avenue
Avenel, New Jersey 07001

A CIP catalog record for this book is available from the Library of Congress.

ISBN 0-517-15942-2

CREDITS

MANAGING EDITOR: Anne McDowall
DESIGNER: Carole Perks
RECIPES BY: Jo Craig, Linda Fraser, Kerenza Harries, Lesley Mackley,
Cecila Norman, Lorna Rhodes, Mary Trewby, Hilaire Walden.
PHOTOGRAPHERS: David Gill, Paul Grater, David Johnson, Sue Jorgensen,
Jon Stewart, Alister Thorpe.
FILMSET BY: SX Composing DTP
COLOUR REPRODUCTION: P & W Graphics Pte Ltd, Singapore
Printed and bound in Slovenia

CONTENTS

INTRODUCTION

The choice of herbs and spices is determined by the place as well as the particular food. We associate chervil, tarragon and marjoram with France; cumin and other curry spices with India; allspice with the West Indies; fresh gingerroot with Asia. And, of course, some spices and herbs are essential to a dish: no self-respecting Italian or Spanish cook would dream of making a risotto or paella without saffron, for instance. Tradition plays an important role in the kitchen.

The traditions are based on centuries of wise experience, and on what is fashionable. This is particularly true when it comes to herbs. Until relatively recently, spices were expensive, highly prized commodities and in some cases worth more than their weight in gold. Products with such economic importance rarely are allowed to disappear from the market place. But herbs have never cost much, and the dividing line between a "weed" and a herbs is a fine one. Dandelion, lovage and salad burnet, for example, were much used up until the end of the last century, then their culinary importance was all but forgotten, which is a pity, as many of the more unusual herbs such as these are excellent included in salads.

Herbs are often added as a garnish. Flowers used to be, and once more it's time to strew them in your salads and on desserts. Good food should taste wonderful and look beautiful.

PUMPKIN SOUP

1 (3-pound) pumpkin
2 tablespoons butter
1 medium-size onion, chopped
2½ cups chicken stock
1 teaspoon light-brown sugar
⅔ cup half and half
¼ teaspoon paprika
good pinch grated nutmeg
salt and pepper to taste
3 slices bread
vegetable oil for frying
paprika

Discard pumpkin seeds and 'strings'. Cut out pumpkin flesh and dice. Heat butter, add onion and cook until soft. Stir in pumpkin, stock and sugar, bring to a boil then simmer for 30 minutes. Purée vegetables and liquid, return to rinsed pan and stir in half and half, paprika, nutmeg and seasonings. Heat through slowly.

Meanwhile, for the niblets, using 2 cutters, 1 a little smaller than the other, cut out bread rings. Pour a thin layer of oil into a medium-sized skillet, heat. Add bread rings and fry until golden. Drain on paper towels. Sprinkle with paprika. Float on the soup.

Makes 6 servings.

CHILLED FISH SOUP

1 pound unpeeled cooked shrimp
3¾ cups water
2 strips lemon peel
2 bay leaves
2 blades mace
salt and pepper
4 small prepared squid, cleaned
green stems 2 green onions, chopped
4 tomatoes, peeled, seeded, chopped
2 tablespoons peeled chopped cucumber

Peel shrimp; reserve. Place shrimp shells, heads and tails, water, lemon peel, bay leaves, mace and seasoning in a large saucepan. Bring to a boil, then simmer 3 minutes. Pour through a muslin-lined sieve. Return to rinsed pan. Cut squid into thin rings; chop tentacles. Add squid to pan and simmer 5 minutes. Cool. Add reserved shrimp, green onions, tomatoes and cucumber. Refrigerate at least 1 hour.

Makes 4 servings.

LEMON GRASS SOUP

6 to 8 ounces raw shrimp
2 teaspoons vegetable oil
2½ cups light fish stock
2 thick stalks lemon grass, finely chopped
3 tablespoons lime juice
1 tablespoon fish sauce
3 kaffir lime leaves, chopped
½ fresh red chili, thinly sliced
½ fresh green chili, thinly sliced
½ teaspoon crushed palm sugar
cilantro leaves, to garnish

Peel shrimp and remove dark veins running down their backs; reserve shrimp and shells.

In a wok, heat oil, add shrimp shells and fry, stirring occasionally, until they change color. Stir in stock, bring to a boil, reduce heat and simmer 20 minutes. Strain stock and return to wok; discard shells. Add lemon grass, lime juice, fish sauce, lime leaves, chilis and sugar. Simmer 2 minutes. Add shrimp and cook just below simmering 2 to 3 minutes until shrimp are pink. Serve in heated bowls garnished with cilantro.

Makes 4 servings.

NEW ENGLAND CLAM CHOWDER

2 (10-ounce) cans clams
3 slices bacon, diced
1 medium-size onion, finely chopped
1 pound potatoes, diced
1¼ cups milk
1¼ cups fish stock
⅔ cup half and half
pinch dried leaf thyme
salt and pepper to taste

Drain clams, reserve liquid. Chop clams. In a large saucepan, fry bacon until fat runs and bacon is lightly browned. Add onion, cook until soft, then stir in reserved clam liquid, potatoes, milk and stock. Bring to a boil, then simmer until potatoes are tender, about 20 minutes.

Stir in half and half, thyme, clams and salt and pepper. Heat gently for 2 to 3 minutes without boiling.

Makes 6 servings.

WATERCRESS SOUP WITH MARIGOLDS

⅔ cup garbanzo beans, soaked in cold water 2 hours
3 thyme sprigs
3 tablespoons olive oil
1 leek, finely chopped
2 zucchini, cubed
1 carrot, sliced
2 tablespoons finely chopped parsley
4½ cups chicken stock
3 cups finely chopped watercress
salt and pepper, to taste
3 marigold flowers, to garnish

In a large saucepan, put beans and soaking liquid, thyme and enough water to cover by about 4 inches. Bring to a boil and boil steadily 10 minutes. Reduce heat, cover and simmer until beans are soft, about 30 to 40 minutes. Drain beans and discard thyme.

In another pan, heat oil, add beans, leek, zucchini, carrot and parsley, and cook, covered, over low heat until vegetables soften, 10 minutes. Add stock and simmer until vegetables are tender, 15 to 20 minutes. Add watercress, then purée pan contents until smooth. Reheat and season. If necessary, thin with a little chicken stock. Garnish with marigold petals.

Makes 4 servings.

MARINATED OLIVES

¼ pound green olives
2 thin lemon slices
2 teaspoons coriander seeds
2 garlic cloves
extra-virgin olive oil, to cover
¼ pound ripe olives
¼ red bell pepper
1 small hot chili pepper
1 fresh thyme sprig

Place green olives in a jar with a tight-fitting lid. Cut each lemon slice into quarters and add to olives. Lightly crush coriander seeds and 1 of the garlic cloves and add to the green olives. Cover with olive oil and seal jar.

Place ripe olives in a separate jar. Crush remaining garlic and cut pepper and chili into strips, removing seeds. Add to olives with thyme. Cover with olive oil and seal jar.

Refrigerate 2 days before transferring to a serving bowl and serving with other appetizers. Consume within one week. The oil can be used for salad dressing and cooking.

Makes 6 servings.

HERB & FETA BALLS

1 cup cream cheese (8 ounces), softened
¾ cup crumbled feta cheese (3 ounces)
1 garlic clove, crushed
1 teaspoon chopped fresh parsley
1 teaspoon chopped fresh mint
2 tablespoons sesame seeds
1 tablespoon finely chopped fresh parsley
1 tablespoon finely chopped fresh mint
grape leaves, to serve
kumquat or yellow tomato wedges, to garnish

In a small bowl, mix together cream cheese and feta cheese until smooth. Stir in garlic, parsley and mint. Roll cheese into 20 balls. Chill at least 1 hour. Meanwhile, toast sesame seeds for garnish: put in a skillet and heat until seeds are golden-brown, stirring frequently. Let cool.

To garnish, mix together chopped parsley and chopped mint. Roll half of the cheese balls in herbs and half in toasted sesame seeds. Serve on grape leaves and garnish with kumquat or yellow tomato wedges.

Makes 20.

CHEESE STRAWS

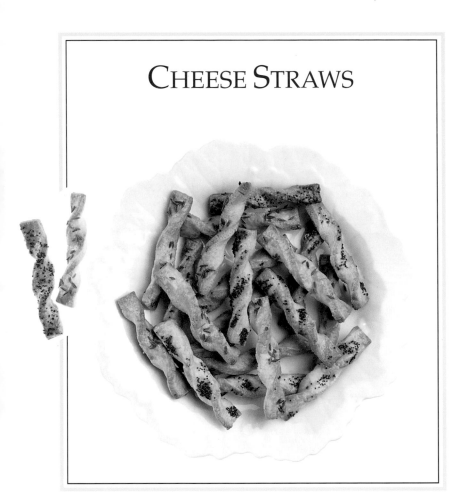

1 cup all-purpose flour

pinch of salt

½ teaspoon curry powder

¼ cup butter, chilled

½ cup shredded Cheddar cheese
(2 ounces)

1 egg, beaten

poppy seeds and cumin seeds,
to finish

Into a bowl, sift flour, salt and curry powder. Cut in butter until mixture resembles fine bread crumbs. Add cheese and half of the egg and mix to form a dough. Cover and refrigerate at least 30 minutes.

Preheat oven to 400F (205C). Butter several baking sheets. On a floured surface, roll out dough to ¼ inch thick. Cut into 3 × ½ inch strips. Twist and place on baking sheets.

Brush cheese straws with remaining egg. Sprinkle half with poppy seeds and half with cumin seeds. Bake 10 to 15 minutes, until golden.

Makes 24 to 30.

POTTED SHRIMP

3¾ pound shelled, cooked small shrimp
salt
cayenne pepper, to taste
1 teaspoon lemon juice
½ teaspoon ground ginger
¾ cup butter
1 tablespoon finely chopped fresh chives
chives, to garnish
French bread or buttered toast, to serve

If using thawed, frozen shrimp, pat dry with paper towels. In a bowl, combine shrimp, salt, cayenne pepper, lemon juice and ginger. Cover and refrigerate.

In a saucepan, melt butter over very low heat. Pour the clear liquid into a bowl, leaving the milky residue in pan to be discarded. Stir chopped chives into clear liquid. Let stand 20 minutes.

Divide shrimp among 6 small ramekin dishes. Spoon chive butter over, pressing shrimp down until covered with butter. Cover and refrigerate until firm. Garnish with chives, and serve with French bread or toast.

Makes 6 servings.

Smoked Salmon Parcels

8 ounce smoked salmon
2 (3-ounce) pkgs. cream cheese, softened
2 tablespoons olive oil
2 teaspoons lime juice
3 tablespoons finely chopped dill weed
black pepper to taste
4 teaspoons horseradish cream
lime slices and dill sprigs, to garnish

Line 4 lightly oiled (⅓-cup) ramekin dishes with smoked salmon, leaving a little extra to cover the top. In a bowl, beat together cheese, oil and lime juice, then stir in dill weed, black pepper and any smoked salmon trimmings. Fold horseradish through, to distribute in strands. Divide mixture between ramekin dishes, cover with smoked salmon and refrigerate 3 to 4 hours. To serve, turn out onto individual small, cold plates and garnish with lime slices and dill sprigs.

Makes 4 servings.

CHICKEN & HAM MOUSSE

1⅓ cups finely ground cooked chicken
1 cup finely ground cooked ham
1 tablespoon fresh lemon juice
1 tablespoon chopped fresh parsley
1 tablespoon snipped fresh chives
⅔ cup mayonnaise
2 teaspoons unflavored gelatin powder
3 tablespoons chicken stock
⅔ cup whipping cream
chives and lemon wedges, to garnish

In a bowl, mix chicken with ham, lemon juice, chopped herbs and mayonnaise.

In a small pan, sprinkle gelatin over chicken stock; leave 5 minutes to soften. Over low heat, melt very gently until gelatin dissolves. Remove from heat; cool. Fold into ham and chicken mixture.

In a medium-size bowl, with an electric mixer, lightly beat cream to form soft peaks. Carefully fold into chicken and ham mixture. Pour mixture into a 4½-cup mold; cover and refrigerate 2 to 3 hours or until set. Unmold carefully on a plate and garnish with chives and lemons. Serve with hot crusty rolls.

Makes 4 servings.

SHRIMP WITH GARLIC

2 tablespoons vegetable oil
5 garlic cloves, chopped
¼-inch slice gingerroot, very finely chopped
14 to 16 large shrimp, peeled, tails on, deveined
2 teaspoons fish sauce
2 tablespoons chopped cilantro
1 to 2 tablespoons water
freshly ground pepper
lettuce leaves, lime wedges and diced cucumber to serve

In a wok, heat oil, add garlic and fry until browned. Stir in gingerroot, heat for 30 seconds, then add shrimp and stir-fry for 2 to 3 minutes until beginning to turn pink. Stir in fish sauce, cilantro, water and plenty of pepper. Boil 1 to 2 minutes.

Line a plate with lettuce; top with shrimp. Serve with lime wedges and diced cucumber.

Serves 4.

MUSSELS
WITH CUMIN

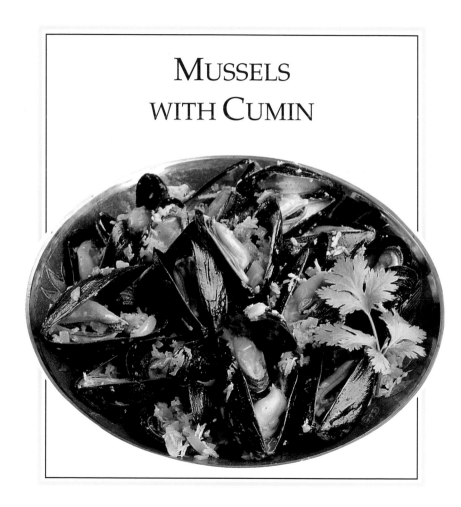

3 pounds mussels

2 tablespoons vegetable oil

1 large onion, finely chopped

6 garlic cloves, crushed

2 green chilis, seeded, finely chopped

1-inch piece fresh gingerroot, grated

½ teaspoon ground turmeric

2 teaspoons ground cumin

1 cup water

1¾ cups shredded fresh coconut

2 tablespoons chopped cilantro

cilantro leaves, to garnish

Discard any damaged and open mussels. Scrub remaining mussels in several changes of cold water, until clean; pull off 'beards'.

In a large saucepan, heat oil in large saucepan, add onion and cook, stirring, until soft, about 5 minutes. Add garlic, chilis, gingerroot, turmeric and cumin. Cook 2 minutes, stirring constantly. Add mussels, coconut and water. Bring to a boil, cover and cook over high heat 5 minutes, shaking pan occasionally, until mussels have opened; discard any that remain closed.

Spoon mussels into warmed serving dish, pour liquid over and sprinkle with chopped cilantro. Garnish with cilantro leaves, and serve.

Makes 4 servings.

Smoked Fish Platter

2 smoked trout fillets, skinned
2 peppered smoked mackerel or smoked whitefish fillets, skinned
2 tablespoons butter, room temperature
1 teaspoon lemon juice
3 slices firm-textured white bread, toasted
1 (3½-ounce) can smoked oysters, drained
small lettuce leaves of your choice
lemon slices and fresh dill sprigs, to garnish
HORSERADISH SAUCE
6 tablespoons plain yogurt
4 teaspoons prepared horseradish
2 teaspoons lemon juice
4 teaspoons chopped parsley
black pepper to taste

For the sauce, in a small bowl, mix all ingredients together well. Spoon into small serving dish. Cut trout into pieces; break mackerel or whitefish into pieces. In a small bowl, beat together butter and lemon juice. Using a small cookie cutter, cut 12 shapes from toast; spread with butter mixture and top each shape with a smoked oyster; arrange on 4 individual plates with fish pieces. Add lettuce leaves and garnish with lemon slices. Serve with sauce.

Makes 4 servings.

GRAVLAX

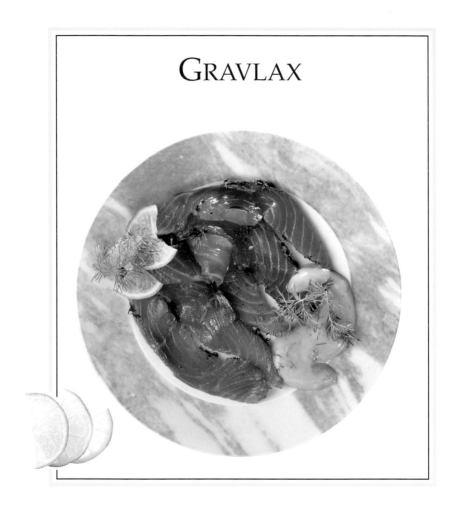

3 tablespoons sea salt

2 to 3 teaspoons light brown sugar

2 teaspoons crushed black peppercorns

6 tablespoons lime juice

large bunch dill weed

3 to 4 pounds salmon, filleted, with skin

lime slices and dill sprigs, to garnish

DILL AND MUSTARD SAUCE

3 tablespoons Dijon mustard

2 tablespoons white wine vinegar

1 tablespoon sugar

²⁄₃ cup grapeseed oil

2 tablespoons finely chopped fresh dill weed

salt and pepper

In a small bowl, mix together salt, sugar, peppercorns and lime juice. In a shallow non-metallic dish, spread some dill weed. Add quarter of salt mixture. Lay one salmon fillet, skin side down, in dish. Cover with plenty of dill weed and sprinkle with half remaining salt mixture. Place remaining salmon on top, skin side up. Cover salmon with remaining dill weed and sprinkle with remaining salt mixture. Cover with parchment paper, then plastic wrap.

Place a two-pound weight on top and refrigerate 3 days, turning occasionally and spooning liquid back between fillets occasionally.

To make sauce, in a bowl, mix together mustard, vinegar, and sugar, then gradually beat in oil. Add chopped dill weed, salt and pepper. Drain salmon well, pat dry and trim off any hard edges. Very thinly slice salmon on the diagonal, discarding skin. Garnish with lime slices and sprigs of dill and serve with sauce.

Serves 8.

FIVE-SPICE SALMON STEAKS

4 × 6-ounce salmon steaks
2 teaspoons five-spice powder
freshly ground pepper
1 tablespoon peanut oil
1 garlic clove, finely chopped
2 tablespoons rice wine
1 tablespoon light soy sauce
1 teaspoon sesame oil
peel of 1 lemon, cut into fine strips

Rinse salmon steaks and pat dry with paper towels. Rub both sides with five-spice powder and freshly ground pepper.

Heat oil in a nonstick or well-seasoned wok, add garlic and salmon and cook 1 or 2 minutes on each side until salmon is lightly browned.

Add the rice wine, soy sauce and sesame oil and simmer 3 or 4 minutes or until salmon is just cooked through. Stir in lemon peel.

Remove salmon with a slotted spoon and remove and discard skin. Serve with wedges of lemon and steamed vegetables.

Makes 4 servings.

CHICKEN BIRYANI

8 tablespoons vegetable oil
1 stick cinnamon
8 whole cloves
6 cardamom pods, bruised
1-inch piece gingerroot, finely chopped
1½ pounds skinned and boned chicken, cubed
2 garlic cloves, crushed
1 teaspoon chili powder
1¼ cups plain yogurt
⅔ cup chicken stock
pinch of saffron threads
¼ cup boiling water
2¼ cups basmati rice
¼ cup golden raisins
¼ cup slivered almonds
1 onion, sliced

Preheat oven to 375F (190C). In a Dutch oven, heat 4 tablespoons of the oil. Add spices and fry 15 seconds. Add chicken, garlic and chili powder and fry, stirring, 4 minutes. Add yogurt, 1 tablespoon at a time, stirring between each addition until yogurt is absorbed by spices. Add stock and simmer 20 to 25 minutes. Transfer to a bowl. In a small bowl, soak saffron in boiling water and set aside. Rinse rice thoroughly under cold running water. In a medium-size saucepan, cook rice in 5 cups boiling salted water 3 minutes, then drain, if necessary.

Wash Dutch oven. Add 2 table-spoons of the oil. Spoon in a layer of rice, sprinkle with a little saffron water and cover with a layer of chicken. Repeat, ending with a layer of rice. Add any cooking juices left from chicken, cover tightly and cook 25 to 30 minutes. In a small pan, heat remaining oil. Fry golden raisins and almonds until golden; remove. Add onion; fry until crisp and golden. Sprinkle biryani with almonds, onion and golden raisins.

Makes 4 servings.

CHICKEN & CORN FRITTERS

1 ripe banana

1 egg

¾ cup finely chopped cooked chicken

1 (8-ounce) can whole-kernel corn, drained

2 green onions, finely chopped

½ teaspoon ground cumin

2 teaspoons chopped fresh cilantro

salt and cayenne pepper

¾ cup self-rising flour

vegetable oil, for frying

chili sauce or chutney

cilantro, to garnish

Mash the banana in a bowl. Add egg, chicken, corn and green onions. Stir in cumin, cilantro, salt and cayenne. Mix well. Add flour and mix to form a soft batter. In a heavy-bottomed skillet, heat oil. Add spoonfuls of chicken mixture. Cook about 1 minute, turning once.

Remove fritters from pan with a slotted spoon. Drain well on paper towels. Serve fritters warm with a chili sauce or chutney. Garnish with cilantro.

Makes 4 servings.

SPICY FRIED CHICKEN

4 chicken breasts
salt and pepper
3 tablespoons paprika
2 tablespoons ground coriander
1 tablespoon ground cumin
finely grated zest and juice 1 lemon
3 tablespoons dark soy sauce
2 tablespoons chopped fresh cilantro
1 teaspoon chopped fresh thyme
1 onion, finely chopped
2 garlic cloves, crushed
1 red chili pepper, seeded and chopped
vegetable oil, for frying
¾ cup all-purpose flour
lemon wedges, to garnish

Remove skin from chicken. Into a shallow dish, place chicken. Make several incisions in chicken pieces. Season well with salt and pepper. In a small bowl, mix together 2 tablespoons of the paprika, 1 tablespoon of the coriander and 2 teaspoons of the cumin. Sprinkle over chicken.

In a small bowl, mix lemon zest and juice with soy sauce. Stir in cilantro, thyme, onion, garlic and chili. Pour over chicken, making sure chicken is well covered. Cover dish with plastic wrap and refrigerate 3 hours or overnight.

Half-fill a deep-fryer or pan with oil. Heat to 375F (190C) or until an 1-inch bread cube browns in 40 seconds. Put flour on a plate; season with salt and pepper. Add remaining paprika, cumin and coriander; mix well. Dip chicken pieces in flour to coat. Deep-fry chicken 15 minutes or until golden-brown and cooked through. Garnish with lemon wedges.

Makes 4 servings.

BROILED CHICKEN
& HERBS

4 chicken breast halves
2 garlic cloves, sliced
4 sprigs rosemary
6 tablespoons olive oil
grated zest ½ lemon
2 tablespoons dry white wine
salt and pepper
½ teaspoon Dijon-style mustard
2 tablespoons balsamic vinegar
1 teaspoon sugar

With a sharp knife, make several incisions in chicken. Insert pieces of garlic and rosemary. Place chicken in a flameproof dish.

In a bowl, mix together 2 tablespoons olive oil with lemon zest and juice, wine, salt and pepper. Pour over chicken breast halves and marinate 45 minutes. Preheat broiler.

Place chicken breast halves, skin-sides down in dish. Broil 5 minutes. Turn chicken over and spoon marinade over; broil 10 minutes longer or until skin is crisp and brown. Beat together mustard, vinegar, sugar, salt and pepper and remaining oil. Add any cooking juices from pan and spoon over chicken to serve.

Makes 4 servings.

MARINATED
CHICKEN SALAD

⅔ cup olive oil

4 tablespoons balsamic vinegar

2 tablespoons shredded fresh basil

2 tablespoons chopped fresh rosemary

2 garlic cloves, crushed

4 skinned and boned chicken breast halves

1 red bell pepper, quartered

1 yellow bell pepper, quartered

2 medium-size zucchini, cut into ½-inch-thick slices

2 large mushrooms

¼ cup pine nuts, toasted

8 sun-dried tomatoes

½ teaspoon sugar

salt and pepper

In a small bowl, mix together half the olive oil, vinegar, basil and rosemary with the garlic. Arrange chicken in a shallow, flameproof dish. Pour oil and herb mixture over chicken; marinate 30 minutes. Preheat broiler.

Place dish of chicken under hot broiler; broil 10 to 14 minutes, turning halfway through, until chicken is brown and crispy. Set aside. Arrange peppers, zucchini and mushrooms in a broiler pan. Brush vegetables with 2 tablespoons oil; broil about 10 minutes, turning once, until cooked. Leave to cool.

Using a sharp knife, peel skins from peppers. Cut mushrooms into quarters. Save any cooking juices from chicken. Slice chicken into 1-inch-thick slices and arrange with the broiled vegetables in a dish. Sprinkle with sun-dried tomatoes and pine nuts. In a small bowl, mix remaining herbs with oil, vinegar and any cooking juices from chicken. Add sugar, salt and pepper; stir to dissolve sugar. Pour over chicken. Marinate 1 hour, stirring occasionally.

Makes 4 servings..

SMOKED CHICKEN KEDGEREE

2 tablespoons butter or margarine
1 teaspoon coriander seeds, crushed
1 onion, sliced
1 teaspoon ground coriander
2 teaspoons ground cumin
½ cup long-grain rice
½ cup red lentils
2½ cups chicken stock
3 cups coarsely chopped smoked chicken
juice ½ lemon
½ cup plain yogurt
2 tablespoons chopped fresh parsley
2 hard-cooked eggs, coarsely chopped
1 lemon, sliced, to garnish
mango chutney and poppadoms, to serve

In a large pan, melt butter. Add coriander seeds and onion. Cook over low heat until slightly softened. Stir in ground coriander, cumin, rice and lentils and coat well with butter. Pour in stock. Bring to a boil, then cover and simmer 10 minutes.

Remove lid. Add chicken and cook 10 minutes longer until all liquid is absorbed and rice and lentils are tender. Stir in lemon juice, yogurt, parsley and eggs. Heat until hot. Spoon into a warmed serving dish and garnish with lemon. Serve with mango chutney and poppadoms.

Makes 4 servings.

MINTED MEATBALLS

1 small onion, quartered
1 (14-ounce) can chopped tomatoes
1¼ cups chicken stock
grated zest and juice ½ large orange
2 tablespoons tomato paste
4 tablespoons chopped fresh mint
1 teaspoon sugar
1 teaspoon red-wine vinegar
1 pound raw chicken, ground
8 green onions, finely chopped
1 cup fresh white bread crumbs
1 small egg, beaten
2 teaspoons ground cumin
salt and pepper
vegetable oil, for frying
Parmesan cheese, grated, to serve
mint sprigs, to garnish

Into a blender or food processor, place onion, tomatoes, stock, orange zest and juice, tomato paste, 2 tablespoons of the chopped mint, the sugar and vinegar. Blend until smooth. Pour into a saucepan and simmer 10 to 15 minutes.

In a large bowl, combine chicken with green onions, bread crumbs, egg, remaining mint, cumin, salt and pepper. Shape into 40 small meatballs. In a large nonstick pan, heat a little oil. Add meatballs; fry 6 to 8 minutes or until slightly browned all over. Remove from pan and drain on paper towels.

Wipe out skillet with paper towels. Return meatballs to skillet. Spoon sauce over meatballs and simmer, uncovered, 15 minutes.

Serve on a bed of freshly cooked spaghetti, sprinkle with Parmesan cheese and garnish with mint sprigs.

Makes 4 servings.

MUSTARD & TARRAGON-COATED LAMB

4-pound boneless lamb shoulder
2 garlic cloves, slivered
4 teaspoons dry mustard
2 teaspoons salt
black pepper to taste
3 to 4 tarragon sprigs
1 tablespoon olive oil
2 tablespoons butter
1 onion, finely sliced
¾ cup white wine
1 tablespoon chopped tarragon
tarragon sprigs, to garnish

With the point of a sharp knife, cut slits in the lamb. Insert garlic slivers. Mix together mustard, salt and pepper. Spread ½ over inside of lamb, and place tarragon sprigs on top. Roll up and secure with string. Spread remaining mustard mixture over lamb.

In a flameproof dish, heat oil and butter, add lamb and brown evenly. Add onions and cook until softened. Stir in wine. Cover and cook in oven preheated to 350F (175C) to required doneness, about 2½ to 3 hours. Pour fat off cooking juices. Simmer juices, stirring, for 2 to 3 minutes. Add chopped tarragon and pour into warmed jug. Cut string from lamb, and carve. Garnish with tarragon sprigs to serve.

Makes 6-8 servings.

CHINESE SPARE RIBS

6 pounds lean pork spare ribs, separated

green onion tassels, to garnish

MARINADE

½ cup hoisin sauce

½ cup miso paste

1¼ cups tomato paste

1½ teaspoons Chinese five-spice powder

1 cup muscovado sugar

3 garlic cloves, crushed

1 teaspoon salt

2 tablespoons rice wine or dry sherry

Trim surplus fat from the pork. In a bowl combine marinade ingredients. Place pork spare ribs in a shallow dish and spread marinade over, turning ribs to coat evenly. Cover. Refrigerate at least 4 hours, preferably overnight.

Prepare barbecue. Place drip pan over medium hot coals, lay ribs on rack and cook 45 to 60 minutes until crisp, turning occasionally and brushing with marinade. Garnish with green onion tassels.

Makes 8 servings.

PORK WITH PEARS

2 tablespoons extra-virgin olive oil
2 onions, chopped
2 pounds boned lean pork, cut into cubes
1 cup red wine
grated zest ½ orange
½ cinnamon stick
salt and pepper
1¼ cups water
2 pears
2 teaspoons honey
chopped fresh cilantro leaves, orange peel strips and pita bread, to garnish

In a flameproof casserole dish, heat oil. Add onions and cook until soft. Push to side of pan, turn up heat and brown meat in batches. Add wine, orange zest, cinnamon stick, salt, pepper and water. Bring to a simmer, then cover casserole and cook 1 hour.

Peel, core and slice pears and place on top of meat. Drizzle honey over pears. Cover pan and simmer 30 to 40 minutes or until meat is tender. Garnish with chopped cilantro leaves, strip of orange peel and pita bread.

Makes 6 servings.

Note: This recipe is traditionally made with quinces. If quinces are available, use them instead of pears.

GROUND MEAT PASTRIES

1 tablespoon pine nuts

¼ cup extra-virgin olive oil

1 onion, finely chopped

1 pound lean ground beef

1 teaspoon ground cinnamon

1 tablespoon chopped fresh parsley

salt and pepper

6 sheets filo pastry, thawed if frozen

Tzatziki, to serve

In a skillet, fry pine nuts in a little oil until golden. Remove from pan and set aside. In the same skillet, heat 2 tablespoons of the oil. Add onion and cook until soft. Stir in beef and cook, stirring, a few minutes or until brown all over. Add cinnamon, parsley, pine nuts, salt and pepper. Cook 10 minutes, then let cool.

Preheat oven to 350F (175C). Cut each sheet of dough into 3 long strips. Brush strips with remaining oil. Spread 1 teaspoon of filling in a line on one end of each strip, leaving a small margin on each side. Roll over twice and fold long sides over the edge, then continue rolling to make a tube. Place on a baking sheet. Bake 20 to 30 minutes or until crisp and golden. Serve with Tzatziki.

BEEF WITH OREGANO

2 tablespoons olive oil

4 strips bacon

2 pounds boneless beef round steak, cut in 10 to 12 pieces

2 onions, quartered

2 tablespoons finely chopped oregano

2 tablespoons finely chopped parsley

1 bay leaf

1 large garlic clove, crushed

$\frac{1}{2}$ cup red wine

$\frac{1}{3}$ cup water

1 cup chopped green olives

2 tablespoons fresh bread crumbs

grated zest 1 lemon

salt and pepper to taste

oregano sprigs, to garnish

fresh bread and green salad, to serve

In a flameproof casserole large enough to place beef in 1 layer, heat oil. Add bacon and sauté until crisp; remove with a slotted spoon and set aside. Add beef and cook until evenly browned. Add onions and toss in oil for 1 minute.

Add $\frac{1}{2}$ oregano and parsley, bay leaf, garlic, wine and water. Cover and simmer 2 hours. Add bacon and olives. Continue cooking 45 minutes – the stew should be fairly liquid.

Mix together bread crumbs, lemon zest and remaining herbs and add to stew. Cook, uncovered, 10 to 15 minutes more. Season with salt and pepper. Discard bay leaf. Garnish with oregano sprigs and serve with fresh bread and salad.

Makes 4 servings.

Variation: Thyme can be added to this casserole for a stronger, more aromatic flavour. Substitute 3 teaspoons finely chopped thyme for half of the oregano.

VANILLA
CRÈME BRÛLÉE

4 egg yolks

2½ teaspoons superfine sugar

pinch of cornstarch

2 vanilla beans

2½ cups whipping cream

additional superfine sugar
for topping

frosted flowers, to serve
(optional)

In a large bowl, lightly beat together egg yolks, sugar and cornstarch. With the point of a sharp knife, slit open vanilla beans and scrap seeds into cream. Heat almost to boiling point. Strain onto egg yolk mixture, stirring. Place bowl over a saucepan of simmering water and cook custard, stirring, until thick enough to coat the back of spoon. Pour into individual gratin dishes. Cool, then cover and refrigerate overnight.

Two hours before serving, sprinkle a thick, even layer of sugar over top of each pudding. Place under a pre-heated broiler until sugar caramelizes. Refrigerate 1¾ hours. Serve garnished with frosted flowers, if desired.

Makes 4-6 servings.

FLAMING
FRUIT SALAD

1 pound (7½ cups) mixed dried
fruit, such as prunes, apricots,
figs, apples, pears and peaches

2½ cups water

2 tablespoons sherry

juice ½ lemon

2 tablespoons honey

½ (3-inch) cinnamon stick

¼ cup brandy

¾ cup toasted sliced almonds

½ cup walnuts, coarsely chopped

fresh herbs to garnish, if desired

Soak dried fruit overnight in water and sherry.

In a saucepan, place fruit and soaking liquid, lemon juice, honey and cinnamon stick. Cover and simmer over low heat until fruit is just tender. Discard cinnamon stick, transfer fruit to a serving dish and keep warm.

In a small pan, heat brandy and light. While still flaming, pour over fruit and sprinkle with almonds and walnuts. Garnish with fresh herbs, if desired, and serve immediately.

Makes 5 to 6 servings.

Note: The effect of flaming brandy is to burn off the alcohol and so concentrate the flavor. It is important to warm brandy first or it will not light.

LAVENDER &
HONEY ICE CREAM

5 sprigs lavender flowers
2½ cups milk
¾ cup lavender honey
4 egg yolks
⅔ cup whipping cream
⅔ cup plain yogurt
lavender flowers, to decorate

Turn freezer to its coldest setting. In a saucepan, heat lavender sprigs and milk to almost boiling. Remove from heat and leave to infuse 30 minutes. Remove lavender sprigs and bring milk back to the boil.

In a small saucepan, heat honey until just warm. In a bowl, whisk egg yolks until thick and light. Gradually stir in warm honey. Pour boiling milk into egg yolk mixture, beating constantly. Pour mixture into a bowl set over a pan of simmering water. Stir about 8 minutes or until custard will coat the back of the spoon. Strain into a bowl, cover and refrigerate until cool. Stir in cream and yogurt.

Pour mixture into a 3¾-cup freezer-proof container. Put in freezer. When sides are beginning to set, beat thoroughly. Return to freezer and repeat after 30 to 40 minutes. When ice cream is just beginning to solidify, beat vigorously to a smooth slush. Return to freezer. Transfer from freezer to refrigerator 20 minutes before serving. Decorate with lavender flowers.

Makes 4 to 6 servings

LEMON GERANIUM SYLLABUB

pared zest and juice 1 lemon

12 large, scented lemon geranium leaves

1¾ cups whipping cream

⅓ cup superfine sugar

½ cup cup dry white wine

2 ounces ratafia cookies (macaroons)

small geranium leaves and lemon slices, to garnish

In a small saucepan, place strips of lemon peel and large geranium leaves. Pour in ⅔ cup of whipping cream. Bring to a boil very slowly, stirring constantly. Remove from heat and cool completely, stirring occasionally.

In a large bowl, combine lemon juice, sugar and wine; stir until sugar completely dissolves. Strain cooked cream-mixture and pour into wine mixture, stirring constantly.

Using an electric mixer, whip until syllabub stands in soft peaks, about 10 to 15 minutes. Divide cookies among 6 dessert dishes and spoon syllabub on top. Decorate with small geranium leaves and lemon slices.

Makes 6 servings.

LEMON &
CARDAMOM CAKE

1 cup ground almonds
⅓ cup superfine sugar
about 3 teaspoons shelled cardamom seeds, ground
½ cup dried bread crumbs
grated zest and juice 2 lemons
4 eggs, separated
pinch salt
whipping cream and shredded lemon zest, to serve

Stir together ground almonds, sugar, cardamom, bread crumbs and lemon zest and juice. Beat egg yolks and add to almond mixture. Whip egg whites until stiff peaks form, then carefully fold into mixture. Pour into buttered 6½-inch springform cake pan and bake in an oven preheated to 375F (190C) until a skewer inserted into center of cake comes out clean, about 40 minutes. Cook in pan, then turn out. Pipe whipped cream on top and sprinkle with shredded lemon zest, if desired.

makes 6 servings.

HONEY SPICE CAKE

⅔ cup butter or margarine

¾ cup packed light brown sugar

½ cup honey

1 tablespoon water

1¾ cups self-rising flour

1½ teaspoons apple pie spice

2 eggs, beaten

2¼ cups powdered sugar

Preheat oven to 350F (175C). Grease a fluted ring mold with a 3¾-cup capacity. Into a saucepan, put butter, sugar, honey and water. Heat gently until butter has melted and sugar has dissolved. Remove from heat and cool 10 minutes.

Into a bowl, sift flour and apple pie spice. Pour in melted mixture and eggs; beat well until smooth. Pour batter into prepared pan. Bake 40 to 50 minutes, until well risen and a skewer inserted into center comes out clean. Cook cake in pan 2 to 3 minutes, then turn out cake and transfer to a wire rack to cool completely.

To make frosting, into a bowl, sift powdered sugar. Stir in enough water to make a smooth frosting. Carefully spoon frosting over cake so cake is evenly covered.

Makes 8 to 10 slices.

GINGER CAKE

2 cups self-rising flour
1 tablespoon ground ginger
1 teaspoon ground cinnamon
½ teaspoon baking soda
½ cup butter or margarine, chilled
¾ cup packed light brown sugar
2 eggs
5 teaspoons light corn syrup
5 teaspoons milk
TOPPING
3 pieces stem ginger
¾ cup powdered sugar
4 teaspoons stem ginger syrup

Preheat oven to 325F (165C). Grease an 11 × 7-inch baking pan and line with waxed paper. Into a bowl, sift flour, ginger, cinnamon and baking soda. Cut in butter, then stir in sugar.

In another bowl, beat together eggs, syrup and milk. Pour into dry ingredients and beat until smooth and glossy. Pour batter into pan. Bake 45 to 50 minutes, until well risen and firm to the touch. Cool in pan 30 minutes, than transfer to a wire rack to cool completely.

Cut each piece of stem ginger into quarters and arrange on top of cake. In a bowl, mix together powdered sugar, ginger syrup and enough water to make a smooth frosting. Put frosting into a waxed-paper pastry bag and drizzle frosting over top of cake. Let set. Cut cake into squares.

Makes 12 pieces.

Caraway Kugelhopf

2 cups all-purpose flour
¼ cup sugar
2 teaspoons active dry yeast
2 tablespoons caraway seeds
¼ cup lukewarm water (130F/55C)
½ cup unsalted butter, melted
3 eggs, beaten
powdered sugar, to finish

Grease an 8-inch kugelhopf mold. Into a bowl, sift flour. Stir in sugar, yeast and caraway seeds. Make a well in center. Stir in water, butter and eggs. Beat vigorously until smooth. Cover bowl with plastic wrap and leave in a warm place until doubled.

Stir mixture and pour into prepared mold. Cover with plastic wrap and leave to rise again until doubled.

Preheat oven to 400F (205C). Bake kugelhopf 20 minutes. Reduce temperature to 375F (190C) and bake 10 minutes longer, until well risen and golden-brown. Cool in the mold 10 minutes, then turn out kugelhopf and transfer to a wire rack. Dust lightly with powdered sugar. Serve with butter while still slightly warm.

Makes 8 to 10 slices.

GINGER
BRANDY SNAPS

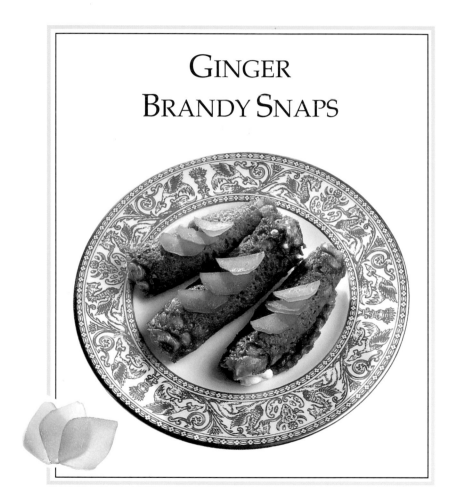

¼ cup unsalted butter
¼ cup packed dark brown sugar
2 tablespoons light corn syrup
½ cup all-purpose flour
½ teaspoon ground ginger
1 teaspoon brandy
FILLING
1¼ cups whipping cream
1 tablespoon stem ginger syrup
6 pieces stem ginger

Preheat oven to 350F (175C). Grease several baking sheets. Butter the handles of 3 or 4 wooden spoons. Into a saucepan over medium heat, put butter, brown sugar and syrup. Heat until butter melts. Cool slightly. Sift flour and ginger onto melted ingredients and stir in with brandy. Drop teaspoonfuls of mixture, well spaced out, onto baking sheets. Bake 7 to 10 minutes, until golden.

Quickly remove brandy snaps from baking sheets and roll around spoon handles, leaving them in place until set. Slide off spoons and leave on wire racks until completely cool.

In a bowl, beat cream with ginger syrup until stiff peaks form. Spoon cream into a pastry bag fitted with a small star tip. Pipe into each end of brandy snaps. Slice stem ginger pieces and use to decorate brandy snaps. Refrigerate until ready to serve.

Makes about 18.

SUGAR &
SPICE BISCUITS

2 cups all-purpose flour
pinch of salt
1/2 teaspoon ground cinnamon
1/4 teaspoon ground allspice
1/4 teaspoon ground mace
1/4 teaspoon ground cloves
1/2 teaspoon baking powder
1/2 cup sugar
1/2 cup butter, softened
1 egg, beaten
GLAZE
1 small egg, beaten
1 tablespoon milk
2 teaspoons superfine sugar
2 tablespoons granulated sugar

Grease several baking sheets with butter. Stir flour, salt, spices, baking powder and sugar together in a medium-size bowl. Cut in butter until mixture resembles fine bread crumbs. Stir in egg then mix with your hand to form a soft dough. If dough is not soft, add water, 1 teaspoon at a time.

Roll out dough on a floured surface to 1/8-inch thickness. Using fancy cookie cutters, cut out shapes from dough. Place on prepared baking sheets. Knead and roll out trimmings; cut out more shapes. Refrigerate unbaked 30 minutes. Preheat oven to 350F (175C).

To make glaze, stir egg, milk and superfine sugar together in a small bowl. Brush glaze over each cookie. Use 1 tablespoon of granulated sugar for sprinkling over glazed cookies. Bake 12 to 15 minutes or until lightly browned. Remove from oven. Sprinkle cookies with remaining granulated sugar. Using a spatula, carefully remove cookies to wire racks to cool. Store in an airtight container.

Makes about 32 cookies.

DOSA

⅓ cup urad dhal or brown lentils
1 cup long-grain rice
12 tablespoons water
2 green onions, finely chopped
2 tablespoons chopped cilantro
1-inch piece fresh gingerroot, grated
1 green chili, seeded, chopped
½ teaspoon salt
about 3 tablespoons water
vegetable oil
cilantro leaves, to garnish

Wash dhal and rice thoroughly; put into separate bowls. Add 2 cups water to each; soak 3 hours, then drain well.

Put dhal in a blender or food processor fitted with the metal blade. Add 6 tablespoons water and process until smooth. Purée rice with 6 tablespoons water in same way. Mix purées together in a large bowl, cover with a damp cloth and set aside at room temperature about 12 hours.

Stir in onions, cilantro, gingerroot, chili, salt and enough water to make a thin batter. Heat a 6-inch skillet over high heat, brush with a little oil, then pour in 2 to 3 tablespoons batter and spread into a 4-inch circle. Cook about 3 minutes, until browned, turning over after about 1½ minutes. Stack on a plate; cover with a dry cloth, while cooking remaining bread. Serve warm, garnished with cilantro leaves.

Makes about 12.

CHEESE BUNS

7 cups bread flour
1 envelope active dry yeast (about 1 tablespoon)
2 teaspoons salt
2 teaspoons sugar
2 tablespoons extra-virgin olive oil
about 2 cups warm water
sesame seeds, to garnish
CHEESE FILLING
12 ounces kefalotiri cheese, grated
4 ounces haloumi cheese, finely chopped
1 tablespoon all-purpose flour
1 teaspoon baking powder
1 tablespoon chopped fresh mint
¼ teaspoon freshly grated nutmeg
4 eggs, beaten

To make the filling, into a bowl, put cheeses. Add flour, baking powder, mint and nutmeg to cheese. Stir in most of beaten egg, reserving extra egg, to make a stiff paste.

To make the dough, into a bowl, sift flour. Stir in yeast, salt and sugar. Add oil and mix in enough warm water to make a soft dough. Turn dough out onto a floured surface and knead 10 minutes or until smooth and elastic. Divide into 16 pieces; roll out each piece to a 4-inch circle.

Place a little filling in center of each circle. Pull dough up on 3 sides to make a triangular shape, with filling showing in center. Pinch corners together well. Place on oiled baking sheets, cover with oiled plastic wrap and leave in a warm place until doubled in size.

Preheat oven to 450F (225C). Brush buns with remaining beaten egg. Sprinkle with sesame seeds. Bake 12 to 15 minutes or until golden-brown.

Makes 16.

FRESH MANGO CHUTNEY

2 mangoes
¼ cup chopped cashew nuts
1 red chili, seeded, finely sliced
¼ cup raisins
2 tablespoons chopped fresh mint
pinch of asafoetida
½ teaspoon ground cumin
½ teaspoon ground coriander
¼ teaspoon cayenne pepper
mint sprigs, to garnish

Very thinly slice mango flesh. Combine with cashew nuts, chili, raisins and mint. Mix together asafoetida, cumin, coriander and cayenne. Stir gently into mango mixture to coat evenly. Cover and refrigerate 2 hours. Serve cold, garnished with mint sprigs.

Makes about 2 cups.

HOT BUTTERED RUM

4 sticks cinnamon
1 tablespoon plus 1 teaspoon light brown sugar
½ cup dark rum
2⅔ cups apple cider
2 tablespoons butter
1 teaspoon ground mace
4 lemon slices

Evenly divide cinnamon sticks, brown sugar and rum among 4 warm heatproof glasses or mugs.

In a saucepan, heat apple cider until very hot but not boiling. Fill each glass or mug to top with apple cider.

Add a dot of butter to each glass. Sprinkle with mace and add a lemon slice. Stir well and serve.

Makes 4 servings.

APPLE & ALE
MULL

2 pounds cooking apples
5 cups ginger ale or ginger beer
6 whole cloves
1 blade mace
1 teaspoon grated nutmeg
½ teaspoon ground ginger
3 strips orange peel
red and green apple and lemon slices

Preheat oven to 400F (205C). Wash apples and remove stalks. Arrange on a baking sheet and bake in oven 30 to 40 minutes or until soft.

Place apples in a saucepan and mash to break up apples. Add ginger ale or ginger beer, cloves, mace, ginger and orange peel. Bring to a boil. Remove from heat and cool. Strain apple mixture through a nylon sieve into a bowl, pressing through as much apple as possible.

Just before serving, return apple and ale mixture to a clean saucepan. Heat until hot enough to drink. Float apple and lemon slices on top and serve in heatproof glasses or mugs.

Makes 10 servings.

BOURBON MINT JULEP

2 ounces bourbon
5 mint sprigs
4 teaspoons sugar
ice cubes
1 dash dark rum or brandy
slice lemon

Mix bourbon, 4 sprigs of mint and sugar in small glass. Pour into glass filled with ice cubes and stir until outside of glass becomes frosted. Top with dash of dark rum or brandy. Garnish with remaining sprig of mint and slice of lemon. Serve with straws.

Makes 1.

INDEX